'Modernity has eradicated the concept of the Holy God from the hearts of most of our youth.'

Ten Proofs for the Existence of God

Hazrat Mirza Bashir-ud-Din Mahmud Ahmad[ra] (1889-1965), the Musleh Mau'ud (the Promised Reformer), was the son of the Promised Messiah[as] and his second successor. He was elected as the khalifa of the Ahmadiyya Muslim Community in 1914 at the age of 25 and led the movement for 52 years. In the period of his khilafat, the message of Ahmadiyyat spread to countries as far and wide as the United States of America and Japan. He also set the foundations of the community's administrative structure and launched numerous initiatives for the propagation of Islam, most notably Tehrik-e-Jadid and Waqf-e-Jadid. A prolific writer, orator and the author of a ten-volume commentary of the Holy Qur'an, he leaves a profound and enduring legacy which lasts to the present day.

Ten Proofs for the Existence of God

Hazrat Mirza Bashir-ud-Din Mahmud Ahmad
Khalifatul-Masih II

TRANSLATED BY
THE FAZLE UMAR FOUNDATION

FAZLE UMAR
FOUNDATION

Ten Proofs for the Existence of God
By Hazrat Mirza Bashir-ud-Din Mahmud Ahmad
Khalifatul-Masih II

Present English Edition: UK 2018

©Islam International Publications Ltd.

Published by:

Islam International Publications Ltd
Unit 3, Bourne Mill Business Park,
Guildford Road, Farnham, Surrey UK, GU9 9PS
United Kingdom

Printed and bound by CPI Group (UK) Ltd, Croydon, CR0 4YY

ISBN: 978-1-84880-911-6

Contents

Note

The words in the text in regular brackets ( ) and in between the long dashes—are the words of the author and if any explanatory words or phrases are added by the translator for the purpose of clarification, they have been placed in square brackets [ ].

The name of Muhammad[sa], the Holy Prophet of Islam, has been followed by the abbreviation [sa], which is an abbreviation for the salutation *Sallallahu 'Alaihi Wasallam* (may peace and blessings of Allah be upon him). The names of other prophets and messengers are followed by the abbreviation [as], an abbreviation for *'Alaihis-Salam* (on whom be peace). The actual salutations have not generally been set out in full, but they should nevertheless be understood as being repeated in full in each case. The abbreviation [ra] is used with the names of the companions of the Holy Prophet[sa] and those of the Promised Messiah[as]. It stands for *Radi Allahu 'anhu, 'anha, 'anhum* (may Allah be pleased with him, with her, with them). The abbreviation ^{rh} stands for *Rahimahullahu Ta'ala* (may Allah have mercy on him). The abbreviation ^{at} stands for *Ayyadahullahu Ta'ala* (may Allah, the Mighty help him).

Because of their frequency of use and for ease of reading, Islamic terms such as *hadith* or *umma* have, for the most part, not been italicised or transliterated in the main body of the text. Anyone interested in the correct pronunciation of these words can refer to the glossary at the end of the book.

All English renditions of the verses of the Holy Qur'an have been taken from the 2004 edition of Maulawi Sher Ali's translation.

Acknowledgements

First and foremost, we owe thanks to Allah Who continues to bless our meagre efforts with His endless grace and favour. Thereafter, this work would not have been possible without the constant guidance and support of Hazrat Khalifatul Masih V (may Allah be his helper) whose instructions, directives and close attention to detail have only helped elevate the quality of all our projects.

I must also thank Nasrah Hamza for her original translation of the text and Mirza Usman Ahmad for his efforts in revising it and for overseeing the project as a whole. Much gratitude is owed to Haseeb Ahmad, Awais Rabbani, Ayyaz Mahmood and Nakasha Ahmad for their elegant proofreading of the text as well as their editorial advice. Further mention must be made of Arsalan Qamar and Syed Talib Mehmood for all their technical and design assistance.

Nasir Ahmad Shams
Secretary Fazle Umar Foundation

Foreword

The quest to find the truth about the existence of God is one of the most fundamental endeavours of human history and the foundation from which other essential questions about life can be examined. Where did we come from? Why are we here? Do our lives have a purpose? What happens to us after we die?

Ever since this search began, oceans of ink have been written on the subject and no less blood has been spilled in seeking answers to the question of whether God exists. From the primitive belief systems of our early ancestors to the sophisticated religions of the contemporary world by way of the philosophical inquiries of figures like Thomas Aquinas, the pursuit of a supreme, perfect and transcendent being continues to this day.

In *Ten Proofs for the Existence of God,* Hazrat Mirza Bashir-ud-Din Mahmud Ahmad[ra] turns to one of atheisms most basic premises—if God exists why cannot we see Him—to undertake his own exploration of this question.

For this, Huzoor begins by demonstrating through reason and logic that sight alone is not the ultimate arbiter of truth, rather human beings are able to determine objects, concepts and information by the other five senses and also through such things as intelligence and intuition.

After demonstrating the falsity of this assertion, Huzoor then turns to the verses of the Holy Qur'an to posit ten arguments in support of the belief in the existence of God. Some of the proofs he offers are similar in nature and content to the established arguments that theists have used for centuries. For example, the intricate complexity of our universe and the idea that something as well-ordered, functional and beautiful must be seen as irrefutable evidence of a creator. Outside of these more traditional arguments, Huzoor also uses other proofs from the Holy Qur'an, primarily the promise of divine support for all messengers and prophets as well as the truth and fulfilment of revelation to show that God exists. Bold, compelling and extensive *Ten Proofs for the Existence of God* is a thought-provoking read which will cause the reader to once again ponder over this most important of questions.

This essay was originally published in March 1913

in the magazine *Tashheez-ul-Azhan* under the title دس دلائل ہستی باری تعالیٰ (*Das Dalail Hasti Bari Ta'ala*) before being reproduced in Volume I of *Anwar-ul-'Uloom*.

بِسْمِ اللهِ الرَّحْمٰنِ الرَّحِيْمِ ۟ نَحْمَدُهٗ وَنُصَلِّيْ عَلٰى رَسُوْلِهِ الْكَرِيْمِ ۟ ¹

اَفِى اللهِ شَكٌّ فَاطِرِ السَّمٰوٰتِ وَالْاَرْضِ ²

Ten Proofs for the Existence of God

Of all the objections raised against religion in the present age by the materialistic world, the greatest are those which relate to the existence of God. Idolaters associate partners with God, but at least they believe in His existence. Atheists, on the other hand, reject the very idea of a deity. The foundations of contemporary science are built on [the principle of] observation; therefore, atheists argue that if there is a god he should be shown to them, otherwise it is impossible for them to believe in him. Modernity has eradicated the concept of the Holy God from the hearts of most of our youth. Hundreds of college students, barristers and other such professionals are turning away from belief in His existence and every day their number increases. Moreover, the hearts of thousands of others are devoid of faith in God, though

---

[1] In the name of Allah, the Gracious, the Merciful. We praise Allah, the Exalted, the Greatest, and we invoke His blessings on His Holy Messenger[sa]. [Publishers]

[2] Are you in doubt concerning Allah, Maker of the heavens and the earth? *Surah Ibrahim*, 14:11 [Publishers]

they do not publicly confess it from fear of societal repercussions. Accordingly, I have long resolved that if God blessed me with the opportunity, I would write and publish a short treatise on this subject in the hope that some fortunate souls may benefit from it.

Atheists primarily contend that they would believe in God if they could see Him. I have heard this argument many times before and it always surprises me since people perceive different types of physical properties through different senses; for example, [some properties are perceived through] sight, others through touch, or smell, or sound or taste. As a case in point, colour is recognised through sight rather than by smell, touch or taste. Hence, if a person denied its existence on the grounds that they could not discern it by way of the faculty of sound, would they not be considered a fool? Similarly, sound itself is perceived through hearing. Again, would it not be ignorant for a person to insist they would only believe someone could speak once they had seen their voice? Likewise, fragrances are known through the sense of smell; yet, if someone were to claim they would only accept the truth of the aroma of a rose if they could taste it, could such a person be considered erudite and intelligent? In contrast, flavours such as sweet, sour, bitter, salty and so on are known by taste and can never be recognised through smell. Hence, it is not necessary to disbelieve in that which cannot be seen and accept only that which is visible to the naked eye. To do this would be to deny the existence of the fragrance of a rose, the sourness of a lime, the sweetness of honey, the bitterness of aloe, the hardness of iron and the beauty of the [human voice]; all of these phenomena are not perceived through sight but through the faculties of smell, taste, touch and sound. Thus the assertion that one has to see God to believe in Him is gravely mistaken. Do such detractors recognise the fragrance of a rose or the sweetness of honey through their sight? If not, why do they insist on sight as the determining factor for belief in God?

Again, there are numerous parts of the human body whose presence we affirm without having viewed them and in fact we are compelled to admit to their existence. Do people believe in the heart, liver, brain, intestines, lungs and spleen only once they have seen them or do they recognise them otherwise? If a person tried to remove their organs in the hopes of being able to see them and prove that these organs existed, they would die before ever getting the chance to see them.

So far, I have cited examples which demonstrate that not all objects are recognised by sight alone, rather some are perceived by the five senses. I will now turn to those phenomena which are known, not through the five senses directly, but by different means. For example, the existence of the mind, intellect and memory is an accepted truth which no one in the world denies; yet has anyone ever seen the intellect, or heard, or tasted, or smelled it? How then was the intellect recognised and how was the existence of memory discerned? There is also strength: an ability which all beings, whether powerful or weak, possess to some degree. But, has anyone ever seen, heard, [smelled], touched or tasted it? Again, how then was the existence of strength established? It can be easily understood from this, even by the most ignorant of people, that such phenomena are determined not through our senses, but by contemplating their effects. For example, when we see people take the time to resolve the various problems that afflict them, it is evident that there is something within them that has assisted them at that moment; we call this thing intelligence. Thus the intellect is not discovered directly through the five senses. Its fundamental truth is determined by witnessing its wonders. Similarly, when a person carries a heavy load, it is clear they possess some sort of capacity which enables them to lift the weight, or to physically manipulate a weaker object; we refer to this as strength or power.

Accordingly, the more refined and subtle a thing is, the more imperceptible it is to the naked eye. Its existence is known through its effects rather than by looking upon it, by smelling it, by tasting it or by touching it.

Hence, when seeking to determine the existence of Allah the Exalted Who is the most subtle of all, it is unjustified to put limitations on the requirements for belief in His existence such as that His existence can only be attained through sight. Has anyone seen electricity? And yet is it possible to deny the truth of electricity when telegrams are sent by it, machines are operated by it and bulbs are lit by it? Modern research on ether has initiated many breakthroughs in the physical sciences, but have scientists been able to discover a method of seeing, hearing, smelling, touching, or tasting this compound? Yet if one denies its existence, the process by which sunlight reaches the earth cannot be explained. Therefore, under these circumstances, it is wrong [for atheists] to ask to see God in order to believe in Him. Allah the Exalted is certainly visible, but He can be observed only by such eyes as are capable of seeing Him. For those who desire to look upon Him, God stands before the world through His strength and power and despite being hidden, He is the most manifest of all. God Almighty explains this in the Holy Qur'an in the following brief yet incomparable words:

$$لَا تُدْرِكُهُ الْأَبْصَارُ وَهُوَ يُدْرِكُ الْأَبْصَارَ ۚ وَهُوَ اللَّطِيفُ الْخَبِيرُ ^3$$

The being of Allah the Exalted is such that eyes cannot reach Him but He reaches the eyes. And He is the Incomprehensible, the All-Aware.

Here Allah the Exalted draws the attention of human beings to the fact that their eyes are incapable of seeing Him for His being is subtle and the finest subtleties cannot be discerned by sight. Power, intelligence, the soul, electricity and ether cannot be seen; how then can the human sight penetrate to the subtleness of God's being?

With that said, how are people meant to see God, and attain knowledge of His being? To this the Holy Qur'an says:

$$وَهُوَ يُدْرِكُ الْأَبْصَارَ$$

That is, He Himself reaches the human eye, and though it is too frail to penetrate to the truth of His

---

[3] *Surah Al-An'am*, 6:104 [Publishers]

being, God reveals Himself to human beings through His power, strength and the manifestation of His perfect attributes. The human eye cannot see Him and so He shows Himself in different ways through demonstrations of His infinite power and strength—whether by way of calamitous punishments, by way of the prophets, by way of signs of divine mercy or through the acceptance of prayer.

If after this explanation, the truth of God's existence is still dependent on observation and it is argued nothing can be accepted until it is seen, then almost four-fifths of the phenomena of the world would have to be denied. And according to some philosophers this would be true for all phenomena, as in keeping with their beliefs, no worldly objects are perceivable, only their attributes can be observed.

I will now seek to present those proofs that establish the existence of God and strengthen human beings in the conviction that they have a creator and are not self-created.

FIRST PROOF

In accordance with my belief that the Holy Qur'an has expounded on all the essential ways to attain spiritual progress, I shall God willing, look only to its verses when submitting proofs for God's existence.

In view of the fact that the first sensory experience a newborn child has of the world is through sound, my opening proof will derive from aurality.

In the Holy Qur'an, God says:

قَدْ أَفْلَحَ مَنْ تَزَكّٰى ○ وَذَكَرَ اسْمَ رَبِّهِ فَصَلّٰى ○ بَلْ تُؤْثِرُوْنَ الْحَيٰوةَ الدُّنْيَا ○ وَالْاٰخِرَةُ خَيْرٌ وَّ أَبْقٰى ○ اِنَّ هٰذَا لَفِى الصُّحُفِ الْاُوْلٰى ○ صُحُفِ اِبْرٰهِيْمَ وَ مُوْسٰى ○[4]

Verily, he *truly* prospers and succeeds who purifies himself, and proclaims the name of his Lord and who not only makes a verbal declaration but engages in worship to demonstrate his belief through his actions. But you prefer the life of this world, whereas the Hereafter is better and more lasting. And this is not an argument presented by the Holy Qur'an alone; rather this indeed is *what is taught* in the former Scriptures—thus the Scriptures of Abraham and Moses imparted this very same teaching to the world.

In this verse, Allah the Exalted sets forth the

---

[4] *Surah Al-A'la*, 87:15-20 [Publishers]

argument to the opponents of the Holy Qur'an that those who eschew selfish desires, who affirm the existence of God and show [themselves] to be His true servants always attain victory and success. And the evidence in favour of this teaching is its commonality among all the religions of the past.

And so, to the followers of the prevalent religions of that era—Christianity, Judaism and Meccan paganism—God makes the decisive argument that the teaching of Abraham[as] and Moses[as], which they all accept, is the exact same teaching. Therefore, the principle that [the loved ones of God always meet with success] and the unanimous agreement of all religions on this teaching and the ubiquity of this truth among all nations is presented by the Holy Qur'an as a great proof of the existence of God.

The more one reflects over this argument, the more convincing and veracious it appears. In truth, all world religions agree on the existence of a being who is the creator of the universe. While there may be differences in doctrines and beliefs because of geographical and circumstantial variances, all faiths universally accept the existence of God even if they diverge on the particulars, such as an understanding of His attributes. All major contemporary religions—Islam,

Christianity, Judaism, Buddhism, Sikhism, Hinduism, and Zoroastrianism—believe in the existence of the One God, *Elohim, Parameshwara, Paramatma, Satguru* or *Yezdan*.

Archaeological evidence also shows even religions now considered extinct were [in their essential features] monotheistic; whether they were found in the far off places of the Americas, the forests of Africa, or in Rome, England, Java-Sumatra, Japan, China, Siberia or Manchuria. How did this harmony of belief arise, and who apprised the inhabitants of America about the creeds of the people of India and similarly who told the people of China about the beliefs of Africans? In the past, [means of transportation and communication such as] trains, telegrams and the post did not exist as they do now, nor were there airplanes or large ships regularly traveling back and forth. Journeys were usually undertaken by horseback or mule and the sailing vessels of the time would take months to complete voyages that now take just days. Vast swathes of the world remained undiscovered during this period. How could a consensus emerge on this particular belief among remote and distant communities of different dispositions and cultures? It is difficult enough for two people to agree on something that has been fabricated;

the fact that so many nations and countries have reached a consensus on a single principle, without any means of exchanging their ideas, is proof of the veracity of this belief which has been mysteriously revealed by Islam and which in the past has been expressed to peoples of all countries and nations. Historians agree that when a claim [or a source] has been affirmed by chroniclers of different [ancient] communities, it ought to be considered authentic. Therefore, when hundreds and thousands of people have agreed on this fundamental precept, why should it not be accepted that they camc to believe in it through some sort of [divine] manifestation?

SECOND PROOF

The second proof forwarded by the Holy Qur'an for the existence of God can be found in the following verses:

تِلْكَ حُجَّتُنَاۤ اٰتَيْنٰهَاۤ اِبْرٰهِيْمَ عَلٰى قَوْمِهٖ نَرْفَعُ دَرَجٰتٍ مَّنْ نَّشَآءُ اِنَّ رَبَّكَ حَكِيْمٌ عَلِيْمٌ ۞ وَوَهَبْنَا لَهٗۤ اِسْحٰقَ وَيَعْقُوْبَ ؕ كُلًّا هَدَيْنَا ۚ وَنُوْحًا هَدَيْنَا مِنْ قَبْلُ وَمِنْ ذُرِّيَّتِهٖ دَاوٗدَ وَسُلَيْمٰنَ وَاَيُّوْبَ وَيُوْسُفَ وَمُوْسٰى وَهٰرُوْنَ ۞ وَكَذٰلِكَ نَجْزِى الْمُحْسِنِيْنَ ۞ وَزَكَرِيَّا وَيَحْيٰى وَعِيْسٰى وَالْيَاسَ ؕ كُلٌّ مِّنَ الصّٰلِحِيْنَ ۞ وَاِسْمٰعِيْلَ وَالْيَسَعَ وَيُوْنُسَ وَلُوْطًا

وَكُلًّا فَضَّلْنَا عَلَى الْعٰلَمِيْنَ ۟ [5]

Several verses later God says:

أُولٰٓئِكَ الَّذِيْنَ هَدَى اللهُ فَبِهُدٰىهُمُ اقْتَدِهْ [6]

That is:

Our argument which We gave to Abraham against his people. We exalt in degrees of rank whomso We please. Thy Lord is indeed Wise, All-Knowing. And We gave him Isaac and Jacob; each did We guide aright, and Noah did We guide aright aforetime, and of his progeny, David and Solomon and Job and Joseph and Moses and Aaron. Thus do We reward those who do good. And *We guided* Zachariah and John and Jesus and Elias; each *one of them* was of the virtuous. And *We also guided* Ishmael and Elisha and Jonah and Lot; and each one did We exalt above the people of their time.

And then:

These it is whom Allah guided aright, so follow

---

[5] *Surah Al-An'am*, 6:84-87 [Publishers]
[6] *Surah Al-An'am*, 6:91 [Publishers]

thou their guidance.

Through these verses, God Almighty asks whether the testimony of numerous righteous people ought to be accepted and given preference to or the claims of uninformed people whose integrity cannot compare with the former. Clearly the claims of those who have, through their character and conduct, established their righteousness and piety and avoided sin and falsehood ought to be given credence to. It is, therefore, incumbent on everyone to follow them and reject their adversaries. Accordingly, we are able to see that all those who, in the past, have spread goodness and established the truth of their piety before the world through their actions, have testified to the existence of a being who across various languages is known as *Allah*, *God* or *Parameshwara*. In India we have the example of righteous individuals like Ramachandra[as] and Krishna[as], in Iran there is the righteousness of Zoroaster[as], in Egypt there was the righteous one of Moses[as], then the righteous Jesus[as] of Nazareth and the righteous Nanak[rh] of Punjab, and ultimately we have the Supreme Leader of the Righteous and the Light of Arabia, Muhammad[sa] the Chosen One, who in his earliest years was given the title of *The Truthful* by his people and who said: فَقَدْ لَبِثْتُ فِيْكُمْ عُمُرًا 'I have lived [all] my life amongst you, can you prove even one lie against me?'[7] And his people did not refute this. All these individuals and thousands more besides have from time to time appeared in the world and declared in unison that there is one God. Not only this, they also claim to have met Him and to have talked to Him. Even the greatest of philosophers who has clearly left his mark in the world cannot present an achievement which matches up to even a thousandth part of the accomplishments attained by these righteous individuals. In fact, if the two were compared with one another, beyond their sayings little would be found by way of deeds and actions in the lives of the philosophers. How can these philosophers compete with the righteous in terms of their demonstration of truthfulness and piety? They teach people to be honest, but do not eschew falsehood themselves. In contrast, those [righteous people] I have mentioned above endured great suffering for the sake of the truth and did not waver even for a moment in their convictions. Plans were made to kill them; they were forced into exile; many tried to humiliate them in market places and alleyways; and the whole world severed their ties with them, yet they

---

[7] *Surah Yunus*, 10:17 [Publishers]

remained firm in their claim and did not resort to lies as a means of protecting themselves. Their actions, their abhorrence for the material trappings of the world, their rejection of ostentation, demonstrated they were selfless individuals whose works were not motivated by selfish desires. Therefore, when such truthful and upright persons have, with one voice claimed to have met with God, heard His voice and witnessed His manifestations, what reason would anyone have to deny their assertions? We accept even the joint testimony of known liars and consider it to be true. Similarly, we accept the reports we read in newspapers even though we are ignorant of the circumstances of those who wrote them. Yet it seems that despite this, we are unwilling to believe the word of these righteous. People claim there is a city called London and we concur; geographers write America is a continent and we accept this truth; travellers say Siberia is a vast sparsely inhabited region and we do not deny this. Why? Because numerous people have given testimony in support of these facts. We believe them in spite of the fact that we are unaware of the circumstances of these people and whether they are tellers of truth or tellers of lies. On the other hand, those who give first-hand testimony of the existence of

God Almighty are such that their honesty is as evident as daylight and they establish truth in the world at the cost of their wealth, their lives, their homeland and even their honour. It is grossly unfair to accept the assertions of travellers and geographers and at the same time refute the claims of such pious people. If the existence of London can be established through the testimony of a few people, why cannot the existence of God be similarly authenticated through the testimony of thousands of righteous people?

In short, the testimony of thousands of truthful and righteous people who have borne witness to the existence of God on the basis of their personal observations cannot be refuted under any circumstances. It is curious that when those who have shared in this experience are unanimous in the claim that there is a God, others who have no understanding of spirituality still call on people to reject their assertions, even though according to [established] principles regarding the processes of testimony, if two witnesses of equal integrity give [conflicting] evidence, the testimony of the eyewitness will be accepted over the other by reason of the fact that while it is possible the latter did not see anything, it is unreasonable to conclude that the former witnessed nothing, but assumed it upon himself that he had. Hence, the testimony of those who claim to have seen God stands over and above those who deny Him.

THIRD PROOF

The third proof which can be ascertained from the Holy Qur'an is that human nature is in itself evidence of the existence of God Almighty, for there are certain evils which human nature inherently abhors. For example, entering incestuous relationships with one's mother, sister or daughter; coming into contact with urine, bodily excrements or other similar types of filth; falsehood and indeed all such other things which even atheists recoil from. Why would this be true if there was no God? If God does not exist, why do men differentiate between their mothers, sisters and other women; why do they perceive lying to be wrong; by what criterion do they assess the above-mentioned things to be abhorrent to them? If their hearts are not in awe of a higher power, why do they shun such things? For them truth and falsehood, justice and injustice should all hold the same value and they ought to act freely in accordance with their inner desires. What is this divine law that governs the emotions and prevails over the hearts of people in a way that even if an atheist denies it with his words, he cannot release himself from his inherent nature and his eschewal of sinful acts or at least his avoidance in disclosing them, is a form of personal evidence that in his heart he too fears having to answer to a king even if he denies his sovereignty? In the Holy Qur'an Allah the Exalted says:

$$ \text{لَاۤ اُقۡسِمُ بِيَوۡمِ الۡقِيَامَةِ} ٥ \text{وَلَاۤ اُقۡسِمُ بِالنَّفۡسِ اللَّوَّامَةِ} ٥^{8} $$

That is, people are mistaken to think there is neither a god nor a final reckoning, when in fact God has manifested two evidences for this. First, all things must meet with a day of judgement in which their affairs are decided. Good is met with good and evil is met with evil. If there is no deity, why is it that reward and punishment are meted out? And those people who deny the Day of Judgement may well be able to witness that judgement begins in this very life. For example, adulterers are more prone to contracting syphilis and gonorrhoea than people who are married even though both engage in the same act. The second evidence is the self-accusing soul. That is, a person's own conscience is able to distinguish sin and identify when something

---

[8] Nay! I call to witness the Day of Resurrection. And I do call to witness the self-accusing soul, *that the Day of Judgment is a certainty.* Surah Al-Qiyamah, 75:2-3 [Publishers]

is wrong or evil. Even atheists recognise adultery and falsehood as wrongs and do not hold up arrogance and jealousy as virtues. Why is this? After all, they do not adhere to any religious law. Instead their hearts are repulsed by certain things—and the heart is thus inclined because it recognises it will face a reckoning for certain actions from a higher being, even if it is unable to articulate this sentiment. In support of this idea, at another place in the Holy Qur'an, God says:

$$فَأَلْهَمَهَا فُجُورَهَا وَتَقْوَىٰهَا ۹$$

And He revealed to it what is wrong for it and what is right for it.

Thus an inherent sense of right and wrong is a magnificent proof for the existence of God. Without God, there is no reason to categorise certain things as virtuous and others as immoral. [In such a case] people would do whatever they wanted, [without any regard for right and wrong].

FOURTH PROOF

The fourth proof we find in the Holy Qur'an for the existence of God is as follows:

---

9 *Surah Ash-Shams*, 91:9 [Publishers]

وَاَنَّ اِلٰى رَبِّكَ الْمُنْتَهٰى ۞ وَاَنَّهُ هُوَ اَضْحَكَ وَاَبْكٰى ۞ وَاَنَّهُ هُوَ اَمَاتَ
وَاَحْيَا ۞ وَاَنَّهُ خَلَقَ الزَّوْجَيْنِ الذَّكَرَ وَالْاُنْثٰى ۞ مِنْ نُّطْفَةٍ اِذَا تُمْنٰى ۞ [10]

That is, God has given to the prophets the knowledge that everything has its ultimate end with Him. All happiness and grief emanates from Him and life and death rests in His hands. It is He Who created both men and women from the emission of a droplet.

In these verses, Allah the Exalted focuses the attention of people to the fact that every action has an agent behind it. It is for certain that whenever an act occurs, there is perforce a performer of that act. Thus if people ponder over the workings of the universe, it will bring them to the conclusion that all things are ultimately caused by God Who is the ultimate or first cause of everything and by Whose command everything occurs. Therefore, God reminds people of their initial state and says they have been created from something [as insignificant as] a sperm drop and the further back they trace their beginnings the more insignificant they become, therefore, they could not have been their own creators. There can be no creation without a creator and human beings are not the agents of their own existence as is evident from the journey

---

[10] *Surah An-Najm*, 53:43-47 [Publishers]

of their progress from a state of weakness to a [state of strength]; therefore, when human beings are not agents of their own creation in their current state, how could they be so in their state of weakness? It has to be accepted from this that they originated from an independent creator whose strength is absolute and whose powers are infinite.

Thus when one ponders over the causes of the gradual development of human beings, the means of this advancement become more and more imperceptible, until a point where all worldly forms of knowledge offer no further explanation or insight into the processes of [these remote stages of human existence]. It is here that the hand of God is at work and all scientists eventually have to concede that everything has a point of culmination and the ultimate end is with a being which cannot be comprehended by the human intellect and that end is God. This is a simple argument which can be understood even by the most ill-educated of people.

It is said someone once asked a Bedouin what proof he had for the existence of God. The Bedouin replied that if he were to see camel dung in a forest, he would be able to tell by looking at it that a camel had passed that way. Therefore, by observing the glorious creation of the universe, why would he not be able to recognise that there was an ultimate creator. What a true and natural response. If human beings ponder over the origins of creation, it perforce leads them to the acceptance of a being who is the ultimate creator of all things.

FIFTH PROOF

Though similar in nature, the fifth proof advanced by the Holy Qur'an in support of the existence of God is far more forceful in terms of the strength of its argument.

Allah says:

تَبَرَكَ الَّذِیْ بِیَدِهِ الْمُلْكُ وَهُوَ عَلٰی كُلِّ شَیْءٍ قَدِیْرُۙۚۥ الَّذِیْ خَلَقَ الْمَوْتَ وَالْحَیٰوةَ لِیَبْلُوَكُمْ اَیُّكُمْ اَحْسَنُ عَمَلًا وَهُوَ الْعَزِیْزُ الْغَفُوْرُۙ الَّذِیْ خَلَقَ سَبْعَ سَمٰوٰتٍ طِبَاقًا مَا تَرٰی فِیْ خَلْقِ الرَّحْمٰنِ مِنْ تَفٰوُتٍ فَارْجِعِ الْبَصَرَ لَ هَلْ تَرٰی مِنْ فُطُوْرٍۙ ثُمَّ ارْجِعِ الْبَصَرَ كَرَّتَیْنِ یَنْقَلِبْ اِلَیْكَ الْبَصَرُ خَاسِئًا وَّهُوَ حَسِیْرٌۙۥ¹¹

Blessed is He in Whose hand is the kingdom, and He has power over all things; Who has created death and life that He might try you—

---

¹¹ *Surah Al-Mulk*, 67:2-5 [Publishers]

which of you is best in deeds; and He is the Mighty, the Most Forgiving. Who has created seven heavens in harmony. No incongruity canst thou see in the creation of the Gracious *God*. Then look again: Seest thou any flaw? Aye, look again, thy sight will *only* return unto thee confused and fatigued.

There are those who say the entire universe came into existence by chance with matter spontaneously forming to bring everything into being. They turn to science to show it is possible the world came together and rotates on its axis on its own, without someone [to sustain it] and make it turn. However, in the above verses, Allah the Exalted answers this contention by saying that there is never a system of design to those things which come together through chance, rather they are marked by disorder. A painting is made using various colours, but if they were aimlessly splashed across a canvas, would a picture still emerge? Similarly, houses are made from bricks; however, if a group of bricks were thrown together would a building still be formed? Even if it is hypothetically accepted that certain things arise from chance, the system and operations of the universe are such that no one can conclude they came into existence by themselves. Let us suppose for a moment the earth arbitrarily emerged from matter and humanity has its origins in chance, but even then, when one looks closely at human creation it is impossible to conclude that such a perfect genesis could emerge from a random cause.

In our general experience of the world, we find that certain features or qualities of objects lead to their creator. When a person views a magnificent work of art, they recognise it has been created by a skilled artist and when a person reads a fine piece of literature they are able to discern it has been produced by a distinguished writer. The more coherent such a work shows itself to be the more apparent the greatness and magnificence of its maker or writer becomes. How then can people imagine that such a beautifully arranged world came into existence arbitrarily and by itself?

Consider for a moment that where human beings have been invested with the capacity for development, they have also been given intelligence so that they can turn their thoughts into action. Further, because human beings need to labour for their sustenance, they have been endowed with such physical bodies as let them move around to gather provisions. If trees require nourishment from the ground, they have been given roots through which they are able to feed themselves;

if lions are carnivorous animals, they have been given claws with which to hunt for prey; if horses and cows consume grass, they were made with necks which could easily bend down and pick at it; and if camels were meant to eat thorns and the leaves of trees, they were given tall necks. Did such a [complex] system emerge arbitrarily? Was chance able to discern that camels would require long necks, lions would need claws, trees would need roots and human beings would need legs? Is it plausible to believe that phenomena springing from chance would result in such a perfect design?

Then if human beings were given lungs, they were also provided air with which to breathe; if their life was made dependent on water, it too was bestowed to them through the sun, clouds [and all other parts of the hydrological cycle]; if they were given eyes, then to help them function sunlight also existed so that they could see by means of it; if they were given ears, pleasant sounds were created; exquisite foods were made available along with our tongues and fragrances were present to stimulate our noses. Chance may have given birth to our lungs, but what brought oxygen into existence? It could be assumed that chance resulted in the creation of our eyes, but how formidable the likelihood of a sun coming into existence millions of miles away to enable them to function properly. Chance may have given birth to our ears, but what power created sound for them to hear; we may accept that dogs and bears randomly came to be found in snow-capped countries, but how did they come to possess such long hair that it protected them from the cold; if chance gave birth to thousands of afflictions, it also gave birth to the requisite cures; chance created stinging nettles which at a touch cause itchiness and it also created spinach as a remedy.

The random chance of atheists is a peculiar thing indeed. It provided for the birth and regeneration of those things that were destined to die, but did not fasten a regenerative cycle to those things that do not meet with [a quick] death. If human beings did not die after their birth, the world would soon have come to an end, hence why death is inextricably attached to them. Whereas celestial bodies like suns, moons and planets do not have a life cycle.

No less astonishing is the fact that because the sun and moon have the powerful attraction of gravity, they are at such a massive distance from one another so that they do not collide. Does not all of this show that the universe emerged from a creator who is not only all-knowing (عَلِيْم) but possesses infinite knowledge? His laws are so perfect, they do not contain any sort of contradiction or incongruity. Even my own fingers appear to me as a proof of His existence. If, with the knowledge that has been extended to me, I had been given the claws of a lion, I would never have been able to write. God gave claws to lions instead of knowledge, just as He gave me knowledge and the fingers with which to record it.

Countless experts and scholars are employed day and night to help improve the governance of nations, yet occasionally they commit such grievous errors that they cause great damage to the state and sometimes bring about its destruction. However, if we accept the workings of the universe emerged from chance alone, it is peculiar to think that thousands of intelligent minds make mistakes, but chance succeeds without fail. The truth is: there is a creator of this universe who is a master (مَالِك) over its entire extent and magnitude. He is mighty (عَزِيْز). Were it not so, such purpose and design would never have been apparent. As the Holy Qur'an says, cast your eyes in every direction and it will become fatigued [from the search]; an order will be manifest in everything. The virtuous are conferred their reward while the wicked receive their punishment. Everything within the universe functions according to its allocated task and does not desist for a moment. This is an extensive subject but I will end the discussion here. For those who have been given wisdom, a simple hint should suffice.

SIXTH PROOF

According to the Holy Qur'an those who reject Allah the Exalted always meet with disgrace and humiliation and this is also proof of their falsehood, for Allah always brings victory for His believers and they enjoy ascendancy over their enemies. If God did not exist, where does this assistance and succour come from? Hence, Pharaoh said to Moses[as]:

فَقَالَ اَنَا رَبُّكُمُ الْاَعْلٰى ۞ فَاَخَذَهُ اللّٰهُ نَكَالَ الْاٰخِرَةِ وَالْاُوْلٰى ۞ [12]

That is, when Moses[as] asked Pharaoh to submit himself in obedience to God, he arrogantly replied: 'What god? It is I who am god.' So Allah the Exalted brought disgrace upon him in this life and in the hereafter. The episode of Pharaoh is a manifest sign which demonstrates how those who disbelieve in

---

[12] Saying, 'I am your Lord, the most high.' So Allah seized him for the punishment of the Hereafter and the present world. *Surah An-Nazi'at,* 79:25-26 [Publishers]

God are always humiliated and shamed. Moreover, no atheist has ever succeeded in establishing a kingdom in the world [in any true sense]. On the contrary, those who have brought about great conquests in the world, reformed countries and created history, have always been those who believe in the existence of God. Is not the humiliation and misfortune of disbelievers and their failure to establish themselves as a nation in the world a matter of great significance?

SEVENTH PROOF

The seventh proof for the existence of Allah the Exalted is that those who believe and have faith in Him and are true in their convictions always achieve success, and despite the hostilities of others they are not afflicted by misfortune. Such individuals as [have been commissioned] to bring people to accept the existence of God have appeared in every country and have met with such an unrivalled degree of opposition that there is no parallel to it. And yet what harm was the world able to inflict on them? Did those who banished Ramachandra[as] find any peace and what riches was Ravana able to attain?[13] Did not the name of

---

[13] An epic poem in the sacred Hindu text the *Ramayana* depicts the struggle between the divine prince Rama and the demon king Ravana.

Ramachandra[as] live on for thousands of years, and was not Ravana's name disgraced forever? Similarly, in what manner were the Kauravas able to profit by rejecting the claims of Krishna[as]—were they not destroyed in the battle of Kurukshetra?[14] The Emperor Pharaoh, who forced the Israelites to make mud bricks, stood himself against a helpless man like Moses[as]. Yet was he able to harm him in any way? Instead, Pharaoh drowned while Moses[as] became a king. The manner in which the world opposed Jesus[as] is common knowledge, and the prosperity that later came to him is also well established. His enemies were destroyed and his followers became the rulers of countries. Our master, the Prophet Muhammad[sa], excelled above all others in the world in his commitment to spreading the name of the Holy God. So much so, a European writer has commented that he was delirious in this, *God forbid*, and the name of God was all that escaped his lips. Seven nations opposed him, both friends and

In the *Ramayana*, Ravana abducts Rama's wife Sita to exact vengeance on Rama and his brother. [Publishers]

[14] The Kurukshetra War, also known as the Mahabharata War, is a battle depicted in the great Sanskrit epic of ancient India, the *Mahabarata*. The conflict was an 18-day dynastic succession struggle fought between two groups of cousins, the Kauravas and Pandavas, for the throne of Hastinapurain. [Publishers]

strangers turned against him and yet the treasures of this world were conquered at his hands. If God did not exist then who came to his aid? If all of this was caused by chance, there should have been at least one prophet who came to establish the eminence of God, but was disgraced by the world. However, all those who have come to elevate the name of God have met with honour and dignity. Allah the Exalted says in the Qur'an:

$$مَنْ يَّتَوَلَّ اللّٰهَ وَرَسُوْلَهُ وَالَّذِيْنَ اٰمَنُوْا فَاِنَّ حِزْبَ اللّٰهِ هُمُ الْغٰلِبُوْنَ ۟ ^{15}$$

Those who take Allah and His Messenger and the believers for friends should rest assured that it is those who believe in Allah that must triumph.

EIGHTH PROOF

The eighth proof found in the Holy Qur'an for the existence of Allah the Exalted is the acceptance of prayer. Whenever an individual supplicates to Him in a state of anxiety, God accepts their entreaties. And this is not specific to any particular period, rather it is true for all

---

[15] *Surah Al-Ma'idah*, 5:57 [Publishers]

times. In the Holy Qur'an Allah the Exalted says:

$$\text{اِذَا سَاَلَكَ عِبَادِیۡ عَنِّیۡ فَاِنِّیۡ قَرِیۡبٌ اُجِیۡبُ دَعۡوَۃَ الدَّاعِ اِذَا دَعَانِ فَلۡیَسۡتَجِیۡبُوۡا لِیۡ وَلۡیُؤۡمِنُوۡا بِیۡ لَعَلَّهُمۡ یَرۡشُدُوۡنَ ۝}^{16}$$

When My servants ask thee about Me, *say*: 'I am present and I am near. I answer the prayer of the supplicant when he prays to Me. So they should hearken to Me and believe in Me, that they may follow the right way.'

Here, a person could ask how we can be certain God is the One Who answers these prayers; why cannot we say the outcomes which emerge from prayer owe themselves to chance as on occasion prayers are seemingly fulfilled, and at other times they are not. If every prayer was effective, such a case could still be made, however, using the example of certain entreaties how can one conclude that they are fulfilled by a deity, rather than the consequence of random events? The answer to this question is that in truth the acceptance of prayer is accompanied by signs. Our master, Hazrat Mirza Ghulam Ahmad of Qadian, the Promised Messiah and Mahdi[as] proposed the following test as a proof of the existence of God Almighty. He suggested a

---

[16] *Surah Al-Baqarah*, 2:187 [Publishers]

set of patients suffering from a serious malady ought to be selected and divided into groups. One set of patients ought to be treated and cared for by doctors, whereas he would pray for the second lot and from this it could be seen as to which patients made the better recovery. What doubt can there be in such a test? Accordingly, he once prayed for the victim of a dog bite who had been struck down by rabies. The doctors in Kasauli[17] refused to treat him and gave a written statement that his condition was incurable. However, through the prayers of the Promised Messiah[as] he returned to health, even though people who are bitten by a rabid dog and have begun to manifest signs of madness rarely recover from it. Thus the acceptance of prayer is proof of the fact there exists a being that answers prayers. Moreover, this phenomenon is not restricted to a particular period of time, rather, such instances can be witnessed in all ages. Prayer finds fulfilment today just as it did in the past.

NINTH PROOF

The ninth proof for the existence of God found in the Holy Qur'an is that of revelation. Though I have

---

[17] Kasauli is a small hill town in the north Indian state of Himachal Pradesh. [Publishers]

placed this at number nine in the list, it is in truth a magnificent proof which establishes the existence of God Almighty with full certitude. Allah the Exalted says:

$$يُثَبِّتُ اللهُ الَّذِينَ اٰمَنُوْا بِالْقَوْلِ الثَّابِتِ فِي الْحَيٰوةِ الدُّنْيَا وَفِي الْاٰخِرَةِ ○^{18}$$

Allah the Exalted strengthens the believers with the word that is firmly established, *both* in the present life and in the Hereafter.

Therefore, when Allah the Exalted speaks to a large number of people across all ages and periods how can denial in His existence be justified? And it is not just that He discourses with His prophets and messengers, but He also speaks with saints and at times, through His mercy, He even speaks to a poor servant of His to bring him solace. He has also spoken to a humble person like myself and confirmed the truth of His existence through His arguments. Further, He even talks with base and wicked individuals to force upon them a conclusive argument of His truth. So, at times, even lowly and evil sections of society experience

---

[18] *Surah Ibrahim*, 14:28 [Publishers]

dreams and revelations, the divine origins of which can be recognised from the fact that they possess news of the unseen which finds fulfilment at its appointed time, and clearly shows they did not emanate from the processes of the mind or dyspepsia. Sometimes, He reveals news of an occurrence hundreds of years into the future so that there is no danger it can be confused with current events which might be seen as having had a bearing on the dream, and which happened to subsequently transpire by chance.

Accordingly, both the Holy Qur'an and the Torah not only mention, but also describe in clear terms, the advancements that have taken place under Christianity today and left the world astonished. Indeed, they also allude to those events that are yet to transpire.

First, we can take the following example:

$$ \text{اِذَا الْعِشَارُ عُطِّلَتْ ○}^{19} $$

That is, a time will come when camels will be made redundant. In a hadith of *Muslim* this is explained in the following terms:

$$ \text{وَلَيُتْرَكَنَّ الْقِلَاصُ فَلَا يُسْعٰى عَلَيْهَا}^{20} $$

---

[19] *Surah At-Takwir*, 81:5 [Publishers]
[20] *Muslim*, p. 78, 2000 Riyadh, Hadith no. 243 [Publishers]

That is, camels will no longer be utilised. In the present age this prophecy has been fulfilled with the development of the railway. The sayings of the Holy Prophet[sa] contain such manifest intimations of this, they are able to conjure up images before one's eyes which make it abundantly clear that the prophetic word was referring to a new mode of transportation that would run with the power of steam and blow mountains of smoke ahead of itself; in terms of its utility and its capacity to load objects it would be like a donkey; it would make noise as it travels and so forth.

Second:

$$ ^{21} \bigcirc \text{اِذَا الصُّحُفُ نُشِرَتْ} $$

That is, books and scriptures would be widely published. Today, because of the innovation of the printing press, the massive extent to which books are now available requires no explanation.

Third:

$$ ^{22} \bigcirc \text{اِذَا النُّفُوسُ زُوِّجَتْ} $$

That is, the fostering of human relationships and

---

[21] When books are spread abroad. *Surah At-Takwir*, 81:11 [Publishers]
[22] When people are brought together. *Surah At-Takwir*, 81:8 [Publishers]

ease of communication is more evident in this age than
in any other.

Fourth:

$$تَرْجُفُ الرَّاجِفَةُ ○ تَتْبَعُهَا الرَّادِفَةُ ○^{23}$$

That is, powerful earthquakes would strike with
more regularity and leave the earth shaken. With
regards to this too, the present age has been marked
by [many such calamities].

Fifth:

$$وَإِنْ مِّنْ قَرْيَةٍ إِلَّا نَحْنُ مُهْلِكُوْهَا قَبْلَ يَوْمِ الْقِيٰمَةِ أَوْ مُعَذِّبُوْهَا ○^{24}$$

There is not a township but We shall destroy it
before the Day of Resurrection, or punish it.

Accordingly, in the present time, numerous
fatalities have been caused by the plague, earthquakes,
raging storms, volcanic eruptions and wars. Currently,
so many potential avenues to death have opened up,
and with such force, that when taken as a whole, no
similar example can be found at any other point in
history.

---

[23] *This will happen on the day* when the quaking *earth* shall quake, and
a second *quaking* shall follow it. *Surah An-Nazi'at*, 79:7-8 [Publishers]
[24] *Surah Bani Isra'il*, 17:59 [Publishers]

As for Islam, it is a religion which has in every century, given rise to such people who have been honoured with divine revelation and who have through extraordinary signs manifested the truth of the existence of a powerful and living being whose intentions emanate from wisdom.

God revealed the following revelation to the chosen one of this age at a moment of great helplessness and anonymity:

يَأْتِيْكَ مِنْ كُلِّ فَجٍّ عَمِيْقٍ يَنْصُرُكَ رِجَالٌ تُوْحِى اِلَيْهِمْ مِنَ السَّمَآءِ وَلَا تُصَعِّرْ لِخَلْقِ اللهِ وَلَا تَسْئَمْ مِنَ النَّاسِ[25]

That is:

People will come to you by every distant track, so much so that the paths they take will become well-worn with use. Men whom We shall direct through revelation from heaven will help you. You should not be discourteous towards those who visit you and be not tired by their large number.

Is this a minor event or a sign to be dismissed

[25] *Barahin-e-Ahmadiyyah Part III, Ruhani Khaza'in* Vol. 1, p. 267 [Publishers]

without due consideration that an individual from a village unknown to the civilised world makes a claim [as the one above], and then despite fierce opposition and constraints, the world witnesses people from America, Africa and all other places gather where he is; the number of these people swells so large that to greet and shake hands with them all is not the task of a normal person; they are a people of great influence, yet they forsake their homeland and take up residence here and the name of Qadian is made famous throughout the world?

In a second instance, a Christian from America called [Alexander] Dowie claimed to be a prophet and published the following vile words:

> I pray to God that Islam should soon disappear from the world. O' God, accept this prayer of mine. O' God destroy Islam.[26]

Only our leader, the Promised Messiah[as], confronted him and published an announcement saying:

> O' you who claim to be a prophet, enter a *mubahala* with me. Our contest will be conducted through prayer and both of us will

---

[26] *Leaves of Healing*, 19 December 1903 [Publishers]

pray to God Almighty that He causes to die first, whichever one of us, is a liar.[27]

To which he insolently replied:

Do you think that I shall reply to these gnats and flies?... If I put my foot on them I would crush out their lives.[28]

But in the same announcement of 23 August 1903, the Promised Messiah[as] said that even if Dowie ran away from this challenge, a great catastrophe would still befall his home of Zion. The Promised Messiah[as] prayed:

O' my God, my most perfect and absolute God, decide this matter quickly and expose the lies of Dowie before the people.

And then my worthy readers let me tell you what happened next. A man who lived the life of a prince and possessed 70 million in currency saw his wife and son become his enemies and his father issued a handbill that claimed his son was of illegitimate birth. He was struck by paralysis and lost his mind to his

---

[27] *The Telegraph*, 5 July 1903 [Publishers]
[28] *Leaves of Healing*, December 1903 [Publishers]

grief. Finally, in March 1907, in a state of regret and misery [he died] exactly as God had revealed to His chosen one and just as the Promised Messiah[as] had foretold in his announcement of 20 February 1907. He wrote that God had said to him:

> I shall manifest a fresh Sign which will bring great victory. This Sign will be for the whole world.[29]

His death was a sign of the existence of God. This was a victory given to the Promised Messiah[as] over the old and new order of the Christian world.

As a third example, let us take the Aryas who dominate over this country and were once led by Lekh Ram. In the booklet *Karamat-us-Sadiqeen* published in the month of *Safar* 1311 Hijri, the Promised Messiah[as] recorded the following prophecy, which he states was given to him as a result of the acceptance of his prayer:

> God has disclosed to me that within six years from today's date this man would be afflicted with great torment on account of his reviling the Holy Prophet, may peace and blessings of Allah be upon him.

---

[29] *Tadhkirah*, p.920, 2009 Ed. [Publishers]

Then in an announcement of 22 February 1893, he foretold the manner of his death:

عِجْلٌ جَسَدٌ لَّهُ خُوَارٌ لَّهُ نَصَبٌ وَعَذَابٌ

That is, Lekh Ram is like the Samaritan golden calf out of which issues a sound that is devoid of spirituality. Hence, he will be afflicted with the same torment that struck the Samaritan golden calf. As everyone is aware, the Samaritan golden calf was cut into pieces, burned and then its ashes were thrown in the river.

Then on 2 April 1893, the Promised Messiah[as] saw a dream in which a strongly built man of hideous appearance—who seemed to be more from among the angels of wrath than from among men—asks where Lekh Ram is.[30] Again in the following verse found in *Karamat-us-Sadiqeen* he also stipulated the date of his demise.

وَبَشَّرَنِیْ رَبِّیْ وَقَالَ مُبَشِّرًا   سَتَعْرِفُ یَوْمَ الْعِیْدِ وَالْعِیْدُ اَقْرَبُ[31]

That is, the day after Eid—a Saturday.

---

[30] *Barakat-ud-Dua, Ruhani Khaza'in* Vol. 6, p. 33 [Publishers]
[31] My Lord gave me the good news and said: You will recognise the day of Joy which will be closest to the day of the Eid. *Tadhkirah*, p.314, 2009 Ed. [Publishers]

Then:

الا اے دشمنِ نادان و بے راہ   بترس از تیغِ بُرّانِ محمّد[32]

Thus five years prior to the event, the Promised Messiah[as] wrote and described how Lekh Ram would be killed. Ultimately, Lekh Ram was killed on 6 March 1897 and with one voice all people accepted that this prophecy had been fulfilled in clear and manifest terms and was a decisive proof of the existence of God.

Thus divine revelation is such a conclusive proof that denying the existence of God in its presence is the height of shamelessness.

TENTH PROOF

The tenth proof identified in the Holy Qur'an to settle each and every issue of contention can be found in the following verse:

وَالَّذِیۡنَ جَاہَدُوۡا فِیۡنَا لَنَہۡدِیَنَّہُمۡ سُبُلَنَا[33]

And *as for* those who strive in Our path—We will surely guide them in Our ways.

---

[32] O' Lekhram why do you revile Muhammad, may peace and blessings of Allah be upon him? Why are you not afraid of his sword which will cut you down to pieces? *Tadhkirah*, p.293-294, 2009 Ed. [Publishers]

[33] *Surah Al-'Ankabut*, 29:70 [Publishers]

All those who have acted in accordance with this verse have always benefited. Anyone who denies the existence of God Almighty ought to bear in mind that if He does indeed exist it places them in a great predicament. Hence, if in the hearts of some people there is a sincere desire to discover the truth, they ought to fall prostrate before God in prayer with full fervour and beseech Him in the following terms:

O' God, if indeed You exist and if, as those who believe in You say, then You are possessed of infinite power—then have mercy on me and guide me to Yourself, and fill my heart with faith and belief so that I may not be left deprived.

If someone adopts this course with a pure heart for at least 40 days, then no matter which religion or country that individual belongs to, the Lord of all the worlds will certainly guide them, and they will quickly see God manifest His existence in a manner that will cleanse the filth of doubt and suspicion from their heart. It is quite clear there can be no deception in this method of finding a resolution. What difficulty can there be for seekers of truth to adopt this approach?

For the time being, I end this discourse on these ten proofs, though there is much more evidence in the Holy Qur'an. However, at present, I feel that this will suffice. If one ponders over these proofs, further evidence will emerge from within them. *And Allah it is Whose help is to be sought.*

In the end, I call on those friends who receive this essay to pass it on to others who they feel might benefit by it after they themselves have finished reading it.

(Tashheez-ul-Azhan, March 1913)

Glossary

Elohim or *Īlohīm* (اِيْلُوْهِيْم) a name for God used frequently in the Hebrew Bible.

Hadith or *Ḥadīth* (حَدِيْث) the recorded sayings and traditions of the Holy Prophet[sa].

Hazrat or *Ḥaḍrat* (حَضْرَت) an honorific Arabic title.

Khalifa or *Khalīfah* (خَلِيْفَه) term used for Islamic spiritual leaders, particularly the successors of the Holy Prophet[sa] and the Promised Messiah[as].

Khalifatul Masih or *Khalīfatul Masīḥ* (خَلِيْفَةُ الْمَسِيْح) title conferred on the spiritual successors of the Promised Messiah[as].

Mubahala or *Mubāhalah* (مُبَاهَلَه) a prayer duel.

Paramatma or *Paramātmā* (پرم آتما) the Supreme Spirit in Hinduism.

Parameshwara or *Paramīshwara* (پرم ایشور) the Supreme God in Hinduism.

Satguru or *Satgurū* (ست گرو) the True Teacher.

Yezdan or *Yazdān* (یزدان) a word for God used in New Persian which has a principle meaning of 'Pure Divinity'.